SERMON OUTLINES
on

The Easter Season

Charles R. Wood

kregel
PUBLICATIONS

Grand Rapids, MI 49501

Sermon Outlines on the Easter Season

© 1994 by Charles R. Wood

Published by Kregel Publications, a division of Kregel, Inc.,
P.O. Box 2607, Grand Rapids, MI 49501. Kregel Publications
provides trusted, biblical publications for Christian growth and
service. Your comments and suggestions are valued.

For more information about Kregel Publications, visit our web
site at: www.kregel.com

Cover design: Frank Gutbrod

Library of Congress Cataloging-in-Publication
Sermon outlines on the Easter season / by Charles R. Wood.
        p.   cm.
1. Lenten sermons—Outlines, syllabi, etc. 2. Easter—
Sermons—Outlines, syllabi, etc. 3. Sermons, American—
Outlines, syllabi, etc. 4. Baptists—Sermons—Outlines, syllabi,
etc. I. Title. II. Charles R. Wood.
BV4277.W66   1994   93-49095
251'.02—dc20

ISBN 0-8254-4120-x

2 3 4 5 / 04 03

Printed in the United States of America

Contents

List of Scripture Texts

Introduction

The Lenten and Easter seasons form a very special time in the church year. So much of significance regarding the life and work of our Lord comes into focus at this time. Suffering and death culminated in His resurrection, and thus the work of redemption was accomplished, validated, and vindicated within the brief span of one week.

The sermon outlines in this book are all the product of the compiler of this collection. They have all been preached from the pulpit of Grace Baptist Church in South Bend, Indiana. Thus they are literally "tried" before presented. Although they are the products of my pen, they all bear the impress of the various sources consulted in their preparation. I am—as ever—particularly indebted to that "Prince of Preachers," Charles Haddon Spurgeon, whose printed sermons are a constant source of mental stimulation and spiritual inspiration.

These messages may be preached "as is," but it is my conviction that their greatest usefulness will be realized if they are carefully studied alongside the Scriptures they seek to expound. Some of these sermons will give rise to several messages in the hands of a thoughtful and creative preacher.

The Bible is the focus of everything in this book. Believing—as I do—that the preacher is bound by the Word of God, each sermon is conditioned by and limited to the "liberating confines" of God's Book.

Thirty-seven years of preaching these great springtime themes has deepened both my understanding of and my appreciation for that great work of redemption, which my Savior accomplished on Calvary and authenticated that first Easter Sunday. May something of my reverence for the Word and awe of the Savior be communicated to you who use this book and through you to those who gather to hear God's Word.

CHARLES R. WOOD

The Cost of Discipleship: Following
Matthew 16:24

Introduction:
What does it mean to be a disciple of Christ? It means following Him. What does it mean to follow Him?

I. **To follow means to go where Christ went.**
   A. Places
      1. Out among need.
      2. To all sorts of people.
      3. Into danger.
   B. Manner
      1. Christ always went to minister.
      2. He was always influential.
      3. He was always dependent on the Father.

II. **To follow means to be submitted.**
   A. Logical
      1. You can't follow one you don't trust.
      2. Absolute confidence is needed for best following.
      3. This is illustrated by a blind man.
   B. Application
      1. We can't say we are really His follower until we are surrendered.
      2. We can't really follow until we are surrendered.

III. **To follow Him means to leave other things.**
   A. Family (Matthew 4:21, 22)
      1. Father likely needed them.
      2. Love for Lord must transcend love for family.
      3. Sometimes will actually involve leaving family (would be temporary and would not often be the case).
   B. Occupation (Matthew 9:9)
      1. It was likely a lucrative profession.
      2. It means that love for the Lord must come before love of profession.
      3. Sometimes it may involve leaving job or profession.
   C. Possessions (Matthew 19:16–25)
      1. Young man had much of goods.
      2. Love for Lord must transcend love for possessions.
      3. Many times it is our possessions that keep us from real discipleship.

Conclusion:

Discipleship requires following—following involves surrender, direction, forsaking. A man must do it in marriage; why not in discipleship?

Denial, Crucifixion, and Discipleship
Matthew 16:21–28

Introduction:
There are certain turning points in Jesus' ministry. One is before us here. "From that time forth began Jesus . . ." He begins to teach about His coming crucifixion and here begins the period of the disciples' misunderstanding which still persist today.

I.   **The Conflict That Clarified the Issue** (vv. 21–23)
    A. Christ's declaration (v. 21).
        1. Something new was introduced.
        2. It was a clear statement of what was coming.
    B. Peter's remonstrance (v. 22).
        1. Peter took hold of him—took him aside.
        2. Rebuke was delivered.
        3. Note very strong language ("God forbid").
        4. Peter's problem.
            a. Could not reconcile this with statement which Christ had just made.
            b. Felt he must continue to be spokesman (probably all others felt this way).
    C. Christ's rebuke (v. 23).
        1. Cut Peter off ("began").
        2. Strong statement—Peter was not Satan but had become his spokesman.
        3. Further detail.
            a. Thou art an offense.
            b. Thou mindest things of men not God.
                (1) Things of God—eternal purposes (musts).
                (2) Things of men—present, visible, obvious.
        4. Implications.
            a. Possibility of becoming Satan's man.
            b. Danger of misunderstanding His purposes.
            c. Peter placed his will before the Lord's because he minded the things of men.

II. **The Correction That Chartered the Course** (v. 24)
    A. The initial condition—"If any man will . . ."
        1. Christ spoke directly to Peter.
        2. It was a declaration of discipleship.
        3. It was a statement of option ("If any man"—there is always an option in discipleship).

B. The detailed demands.
   1. Let him deny himself.
      a. It was more than common term for self-denial.
      b. He is to renounce himself as the great object of concern and attention.
   2. Let him take up his cross.
      a. Common for malefactors to carry own cross.
      b. Basest form of suffering.
      c. Meaning—to cheerfully bear the suffering, shame, and loss directly connected with our following of Christ.
      d. Luke adds "daily" (Luke 9:23).
   3. Let him follow Me.
      a. More than just going after Him—already said that.
      b. "Let him pattern his life on mine."
      c. In contrast to what Peter has just done.
C. The present implications.
   1. We are faced with discipleship option.
   2. It involves the three elements mentioned.
   3. We are too much minded with the things of this world.

III. The Reasons That Ramify the Requirements (vv. 25–27)
A. The first reason (v. 25).
   1. Proverbial expression.
   2. "Life" the natural, human.
   3. Meaning.
      a. The one who sets up physical as ultimate will only lose.
      b. The one who counts physical as little will find the real life.
   4. Be a disciple because the physical life is not the lasting life; the spiritual is.
B. The second reason (v. 26).
   1. Taken from the world of commerce.
   2. It is twofold.
      a. What's the use of winning the world and losing the soul?
      b. What can a man swap for his soul (Faust).
   3. Be a disciple because of the overwhelming importance of the soul.
C. The third reason (v. 27).
   1. It is a prediction of the second coming.
   2. Christ is coming in glory but also in power.

3. He is coming to bring rewards.
4. Be a disciple because He is going to come and reward us for the way we live.

Conclusion:

Christ teaches about the nature of His kingdom. Peter intrudes the things of this world into it. Christ delineates the demands and then presents reasons. Have you been playing Peter? Christ issues a warning: "Get thee behind me . . ."

The Cost of Discipleship: Self-denial
Matthew 16:24

Introduction:
We note a change in emphasis in Christ's ministry at this point. He begins to center on the cross. He knows that all will be offended in Him, and He tries to prepare them for it. His teaching lays stress on the fact that it costs to be His disciple.

I. **The Conditional Element**
   A. If any seeks to follow the Lord.
   B. Emphasis is on any—non-restrictive.
   C. "Come after"—story of James and John leaving and following—is true today in different ways.

II. **The Demand Element**
   A. "Deny"—Refuse to own—say "no" to (e.g. Peter in the hall of judgment).
   B. What is the object?
      1. We like to fill in things.
      2. "Himself" is the object.
   C. The implications.
      1. Denial of things I want.
      2. Denial of my rights.
      3. Denial of self-expression.
      4. Denial of fleshly desires.
      5. Denial of life centered in the flesh.

III. **The Example Element**
   A. Best exemplified in Christ Himself.
   B. Specific instances.
      1. His agony in the garden.
      2. "He could have called ten thousand angels."
      3. His coming in the first place (Phil. 2).

Conclusion:
There is so much misunderstanding of Christianity. Do you really wish to follow Him, or are you just content to be in the orb of safety? There is no such thing as "just saved." Some may be ignorant of the demands of Christ. Once known, however, failure to follow is sinful disobedience.

Strategy, Seductions, and Suppositions
Matthew 4:2–3

Introduction:
Christ lived His life under specific Satanic attack. As His children we can expect the same thing.

I. **Satan's Strategy**
   A. Keep Christ from the cross.
      1. It began from the time of His birth.
      2. Satan used every possible means.
   B. Keep from rising once He got to cross.
      1. Tried to be sure He was dead.
      2. Tried to be sure He stayed that way.
   C. Keep people from receiving Him once He rose.
      1. Again uses every possible means.
      2. Even builds elaborate alternative religions.
   D. Keep people from relating to Him if they receive Him.
      1. He is constantly after our relationship.
      2. This is the area of the first temptation.

II. **Specific Seductions** (appeals in the first temptation)
   A. Questions God's Word.
      1. "If Thou be . . ." (note 3:17).
      2. Reminds of fall—"yea, hath God said?"
   B. Questions God's relationship to the Son.
      1. "If Thou be the Son of God," then why are you in this condition? (hungry and exhausted)
      2. If Satan can shake the relationship, then
         a. He can eliminate dependence on the Father.
         b. He can eliminate duty to Him.
         c. He can eliminate communion with Him.
         d. He can keep Christ off the cross.
   C. Questions God's goodness.
      1. "If Thou be the Son of God," and in this condition? (hungry and exhausted)
      2. Satan insinuated hard thoughts of God (Satan is unkind, unfaithful, forgetful, and tends to forsake).
   D. Suggests acting according to His own will.
      1. Nothing wrong in making stones into bread.
      2. Wrong was in taking things into His own hands.
      3. This would show lack of trust in the Father.

III. **Significant Suppositions**
    A. Satan is more subtle than you suppose.
       1. Note he uses neutral action here.
       2. Uses every possible means to hinder.
    B. Sin is much more mental than physical.
       1. He attacked the mind of Christ.
       2. If he gets our minds, he will get our actions.
    C. Sin is broader in scope than usually allowed.
       1. Some allowable acts rendered sinful by thoughts.
       2. Answers, "I haven't sinned all day."
    D. Action is revealer of thoughts and attitudes.
       1. Why we do things incredibly important.
       2. Only individual can finally determine.

Conclusion:

There are many faces of temptation! Sometimes it comes as a seductive person, iridescent cash, or an overwhelming drive for self-preservation. Other times it comes as a quiet voice in time of trouble questioning the truth of God's promises, questioning the reality of Christianity, questioning the goodness of God, urging us to take matters into our own hands. Satan says, "Yea, hath God said?" "Are you really a child of God?" "Isn't God somewhat hard on you?" "Why not do ___?" Beware of Satan's strategies, seductions, and suppositions.

The Hypocrite's Hypocrite
Matthew 27:3–10; Acts 1:15–19

Introduction:
"There are too many hypocrites in the church." Unfortunately, that's a true statement, but there are hypocrites in all of life. Hypocrisy needs to be faced and dealt with, and Judas may help us to do that.

I. **The Hypocrisy of Judas**
  A. Seen in the fact that none of the disciples suspected him.
    1. Nothing negative was said while he was among them.
    2. All negative comments were "after the fact."
  B. Seen in his reaction to Mary's anointing of Christ (John 12:2–6).
    1. He complained about waste but sold Christ for much less.
    2. His motives are spelled out by John.
  C. Seen is his purchase of land—what did he do with the money?
    1. Land mentioned in Acts 2 is different from that in Matthew 27.
      a. He owned land where he went to commit suicide.
      b. Priests bought piece of land for burial.
    2. He was putting skimmed money to good use.

II. **The Lessons of the Hypocrisy of Judas**
  A. It's a matter of a mask.
    1. Acting a part (using a mask in Greek drama).
    2. Acting a part for a base end or giving one's self out to be what one really isn't.
  B. It's a matter of manner.
    1. Judas must have spoken and acted exactly like everyone else.
    2. There was nothing in his manner to expose him.
    3. This is not always the case—some hypocrites are obvious.
  C. It's a matter of method—usual one is misleading.
    1. Seen in Judas's words about feeding the poor.
    2. Attempts are often made to divert attention.

3. Hypocrisy usually involves some attempt to divert attention from the real issue to something else.
D. It's a matter of motive.
   1. Hypocrisy made worse when it is intentional.
      a. We are all hypocritical to some degree.
      b. When we are deliberately so, it is worse.
   2. Hypocrisy is hypocrisy in spite of motives.
      a. Takes away shelter.
      b. Many hypocrites convince themselves of the purity of their motives.
   3. Our motives are always mixed.
      a. Remember about the heart...
      b. We need to examine what we are doing.
E. It's a matter of madness.
   1. Led to Judas's condemnation.
      a. Christ saw through it from the beginning.
      b. Resulted in disgrace and death.
   2. Keeps or leads away from God.
   3. Will always be ultimately exposed.

Conclusion:

Christians are frequently guilty of hypocrisy, but unconverted people are just as guilty. Judas is one example of hypocrisy in the Bible. David is another example of hypocrisy. David found forgiveness; Judas did not. David confessed his sin and repented of his hypocrisy; Judas merely expressed sorrow for the mess he had made.

So Near and Yet So Far

John 12:1–8

Introduction:

Notice the scene: Christ is approaching the last week of His life. He is in Bethany again, a suburb of Jerusalem. He is with the family of Lazarus, Mary, and Martha plus others. He is enjoying a meal when Mary leaves the table. She gets a box of ointment, anoints His feet, and wipes the excess away with her hair. Notice the response of Judas as it reveals so much.

I. **He Never Had an Idea of What Was Going On**
    A. What was revealed by her action.
        1. Who Christ truly was.
        2. The real character of gratitude.
        3. The quality of sacrifice.
        4. The full measure of loving devotion.
        5. The effects of true spontaneity.
        6. The purpose of possessions.
    B. Judas missed all of what was happening here.
        1. He knew less than the rest of the disciples.
        2. His motives were wrong, but the point is that he missed out.
    C. People miss the whole point today.
        1. Those who attend only occasionally.
        2. Those who only attend and are not involved.
        3. Those who never participate or serve.
        4. Those who mainly come to criticize.

II. **He Became a Spokesman for Satan**
    A. His criticism is an attack on Christ.
        1. In this he is speaking for Satan.
        2. He was a disciple, a preacher.
    B. Seems like a strong statement, but Peter did it (Matt. 16:33).
        1. Incident follows confession of faith.
        2. Christ says exactly what He said to Satan (Luke 4:8).
        3. Both Peter and Judas speak for Satan.
    C. This still happens today.
        1. Just because a person is a Christian or even a preacher doesn't mean he can't deny Christ on occasion.
        2. The Word of God is the test—we need to use it!

III. He Was Never Saved
    A. Very obvious from Scripture.
        1. John 6:70—"Have I not chosen you twelve, and one of you is a devil?"
        2. Statements at last supper (John 12:2, 10–11).
    B. Jesus appears to be only one who knows this.
        1. Rest of disciples appear to consider him one of them.
        2. No indication of any kind there was any knowledge of Judas's real character until after the resurrection.
        3. "He was one with their number but not with their nature."
    C. This is still possible today.
        1. Don't subscribe to idea that most church members are not saved.
        2. Still know this situation is possible—key issue: are you saved and sure of it?

Conclusion:

No one names his child Judas! Everyone is afraid of him, and all should be. He shows you can be in the "in" group and still not have any idea about what's really going on. If Judas speaks to your heart, you need to do something about it!

Motivated by Money
John 12:6; 18:2–9

Introduction:

The writers of "Jesus Christ, Superstar" paint a positive portrait of Judas. It is not a new portrait. Judas was a man of like passions as we (covetous, jealous, ambitions) who allowed those passions to gain control of his life and its course.

I. **The Covetousness of Judas**
   A. Shown in connection with Mary's act of gratitude (John 12:6).
      1. Complained because ointment not sold to benefit poor.
      2. John gives real reason for complaint.
         a. He was the treasurer.
         b. He was a thief at heart.
         c. He "bare away" what was put in the bag.
   B. Shown by his betrayal of Jesus (John 18:2–3).
      1. What happened here?
         a. Misperception—He would hide; Judas knew where.
         b. Roman soldiers present to assure safety, but they would not know Him.
         c. He would hide behind others—thus kiss sign from Judas .
      2. Why did Judas do it?
         a. Maybe: no kingdom; wanted to "cut himself a deal."
         b. Money amount moderate (price of slave) .
         c. Judas may have felt it was best he could do.
   C. Shown by his remorse (Matt. 27:3–10).
      1. Money was the issue.
         a. Shown by Judas's reaction.
         b. Shown by prominence of money in the story.
      2. Judas's repentance was flawed.
         a. Sorry for mess caused but not for what he had done.
         b. "Judas was bad enough to betray Christ, but good enough to wish he hadn't."
   D. The results of his covetousness are obvious.
      1. He was directed by money—increasingly a determining influence in his life.

2. He then became dominated by it—probably never intended at the start to betray Jesus.
3. He was finally destroyed by it—death by suicide was an ignominious end!

II. The Motivation of Money
A. It determines our values.
   1. Money can profoundly influence our right/wrong decisions.
   2. We tend to have a "money cap"—above which the rules change.
   3. Money never rightly determines our values.
B. It defines our priorities.
   1. All have priority system and have assigned positions on it.
   2. Money tends to cloud our priorities, put income production before mate, family, church, and even personal health.
   3. Money is *a* factor, not *the* factor in prioritizing.
C. It directs our decisions.
   1. A consideration in determining the Lord's will.
   2. Becomes the determinant of God's will in many cases.
   3. If it is God's will, there will be adequate finances for it.

III. The Answer to Being Moved by Money
A. Seek—seek *first* the kingdom of God and His righteousness.
   1. That which contributes to His rule and reign.
   2. That which is in accord with righteousness.
B. Settle—the issue of money.
   1. Decide what money means to you.
   2. Come to terms with the grip money has on you.
C. Structure—get your financial life in order.
   1. Many money problems come from mismanagement.
   2. Practice biblical principles.
D. Secure—your soul ("For what shall it profit a man if he gain the whole world and lose his own soul").

Conclusion:

Judas is a sad story as he allowed covetousness to direct, dominate, and destroy him. We must be sure we have dealt with covetousness.

What does, "Seek ye first . . ." mean to you?

Have you settled the issue of money in your life?

Is your financial life structured according to Scripture?

Have you secured your soul?

A Cracked Mirror

John 13:21–31

Introduction:
My hair is such that I often need a mirror, and I find myself looking at some amazing things seeking a reflection. No matter how flawed, something is better than nothing. Judas was flawed to the ultimate degree, but he does serve as a mirror that reflects two very important things.

I. **Judas Reflects Human Depravity** (A graphic illustration of Jer. 17:9)
   A. The tendency to miss opportunity.
      1. He was constantly faced with tremendous opportunity.
      2. He wasted those opportunities along with his natural gifts and his life.
      3. He is proof that no gifts can ensure grace.
      4. He was blinded to the true value of life.
   B. The temptation of half-hearted following.
      1. He was never really committed to Christ.
      2. He shows how close one can be and still be lost.
   C. The power of covetousness.
      1. He was "mastered by money" (Matt. 26:15).
      2. He didn't forsake his "master"—he served it faithfully.
   D. The degenerative process of sin.
      1. Sin's hold grows gradually: guest, friend, master.
      2. Sin caused him to go against trust and confidence.
      3. Sin made him fail to hear repeated warnings.
      4. Sin brought him to seek out his own temptation.
   E. The inadequacy of conscience.
      1. He evidently had one—something caused him to hang himself.
      2. His conscience was not sufficient to keep him from trouble.

II. **Judas Reflects Divine Graciousness**
   A. Notice Christ's knowledge of Judas.
      1. He knew who he was—predicted betrayer.
      2. He knew what he was—an unbeliever in the group.
      3. He knew what he would do—in significant detail.
   B. Notice Christ's treatment of Judas.
      1. Gave him repeated warnings in His teaching.

2. Incredible story of final night.
   a. Kissed him upon entry (custom).
   b. Gave him seat of honor on left hand.
   c. Washed his feet.
   d. Gave him sop—token of friendship.
   e. Spoke words of warning (John 13:10–11).
   f. Used quotation identifying him (Jn. 13:18; Ps. 41:9).
   g. Spoke final word of warning (Matt. 26:24).
3. Until the very end Jesus protected Judas and gave him opportunity to repent.
4. Judas could doubtlessly have found forgiveness and restoration even at the end.
C. Notice Christ's example with Judas.
   1. His kindness and courtesy to him.
      a. Judas was unbeliever.
      b. We have trouble with brothers with whom we disagree.
   2. His concern for an unbeliever.
   3. His tremendous love for the lost.
      a. If you have never trusted Him, He loves you.
      b. No matter what you have done, He loves you.

Conclusion:

Judas speaks loudly and clearly and says, "Don't trust yourself!" Judas also becomes a mirror reflecting the graciousness of a loving Lord. Have you experienced His grace? If not, why not? If not, when?

The Great Palm Sunday Caper
John 12:12–19

Introduction:
Palm Sunday is difficult to understand. What exactly was going on? What was Jesus actually doing? What was with the crowd? How could the same group of people shout "Hosannah" on Sunday and "Crucify Him" later in the week? Let's try to answer those questions.

I. **Reasons for the Reversal**
    A. Different crowds in view.
        1. City was crowded with pilgrims for Passover.
        2. Enough people that crowds could have been somewhat different.
        3. Crowd that had been at Bethany also mentioned (v. 17).
        4. Really inconceivable that entire crowd would be different.
    B. The fickleness of crowds in general.
        1. "One day a hero, next day a bum" very common.
        2. This was obviously an agitated crowd (leaders were "working" it).
        3. Certain types of crowds were easily swayed.
        4. Better type crowd here considering all the pilgrims. Difficult to accept that this was solely due to fickleness.
    C. Hypocrisy in acclaim.
        1. They were not sincere in what they said.
        2. There was a measure of mockery in their statements.
        3. They were simply looking for something to entertain them.
        4. Quotation of Scripture and tenor of record make this difficult to accept.
    D. Genuine misunderstanding.
        1. They were looking for a Messiah.
        2. They had certain criteria for the One who would come: political strength, military prowess, personal charisma, activism.
        3. As soon as the event begin to unfold, they realize that their expectations had been mistaken.
        4. Disappointment always makes it easier to turn on someone.

II. Lessons in the Reversal
   A. People today do no better at understanding Him.
      1. Many do not know Who He is.
      2. Even more are confused about His roles.
   B. The main groups of the confused.
      1. Those who do not accept His deity.
      2. Those who have unrealistic expectations regarding Him: note some of the false claims being made today.
      3. Those who do not recognize Him as Savior.
      4. Those who do not recognize Him as Lord.

Conclusion:

The problem of the Palm Sunday crowd was one of misunderstanding. They thought He was something He wasn't because they didn't know who He was. If He were to come to our town today, the same thing would happen. Do you really understand Who He is?

Of Kings and Colts

Matthew 21:1–11

Introduction:
Palm Sunday is an easy scene to recreate. It is so very familiar, but what really is going on here?

I.   **The Issues**—We must understand . . .
   A. Occupied nation syndrome.
      1. Romans despised Jews and made life difficult.
      2. Jews hated Romans and rankled under them.
   B. Messianic expectations.
      1. Promise of O.T.
      2. What better time than this?
   C. Raising of Lazarus.
      1. Had just taken place.
      2. Was well known to all.
      3. Brought things to a head.

II. **The Intention**—Why did this happen?
   A. It was not just to fulfill prophecy.
      1. Things didn't happen just for that.
      2. Events prophesied because coming.
   B. Christ takes control of own destiny.
      1. Deliberately precipitates crisis.
         a. Takes matters into own hands.
         b. Forces issue.
      2. Brought events to God's timing.
         a. Whole matter is in hands of God.
         b. Crucial event.

III. **The Identifications**
   A. Actions of Christ.
      1. Sets self forth as Messiah.
      2. Colt shows what sort of Messiah.
   B. Responses to Him.
      1. Leaders completely missed point (asked Him to quiet the crowd).
      2. People no less miss point.
         a. They linked Him to Psalms.
         b. They should have linked Him to the rest of O.T.

C. Explanation of crowd's turn.
   1. They were fickle.
   2. They expected a political Messiah.
      a. He showed He was not such.
      b. They became disillusioned.

IV. The Implications
   A. God is in control of every timetable.
   B. Beware of "Protestations of Praise."
   C. People want kingdom on own terms.
      1. "Health, wealth, prosperity" view wants that kind of kingdom.
      2. Those who want Him as Savior but not as Lord.
      3. Those who want salvation some other way.

Conclusion:
If Christ should come riding into your town today, how would you respond?

Just a Donkey Colt
Matthew 21:1–11

Introduction:
The small details of Scripture are not accidental or even incidental. Everything is done for a reason and with a purpose. One of the small details of Palm Sunday is the animal involved, the donkey colt on which Christ rode. This animal is not at all incidental to the story.

I. **Donkey Colt Representative of His Ministry**
   A. Kings, great men, warriors normally rode horses.
   B. A donkey is humble, meek, unassuming, simple.
   C. Provided perfect likeness for Christ.
      1. "My kingdom is not of this world."
      2. Statement has incredible implications for followers.

II. **Donkey Colt Had Never Been Ridden Before**
   A. There are several factors here.
      1. Probably explains why Matthew speaks of the donkey as well as the colt.
      2. Old Testament sacred services reserved for animals which had not been under the yoke.
      3. Shows Christ's rule over the natural world.
   B. Fitting as this was something new.
      1. Men had died for the gods before; never had God died for men.
      2. Complete fulfillment of Old Testament system in something new.

III. **Donkey Colt Was Burden Bearing Animal**
   A. Donkeys were . . .
      1. Not for status but for service.
      2. Not for battle but for burdens.
   B. They are a perfect reflection of Christ's ministry.
      1. He came to bear people's burdens.
      2. He bore the ultimate burden—sin.

IV. **Donkey Colt Was Borrowed**
   A. Everything He had on earth was borrowed (stable, boat, quarters, even the tomb).
      1. He owned all things but possessed nothing.
      2. We possess all things but own nothing.

B. Note from the story:
1. There are always those who are willing to help the work of the Lord.
2. Even the most humble can serve the highest.
3. When He asks for it, the answer is "yes."
   a. "We spoil so much of our obedience by criticizing the things we are called to do, be, or bear."
   b. "Then we hesitate, question, doubt, and do languidly at last what to do."

Conclusion:

The choice of an animal was just a little detail, but it was a perfect choice. Have you accepted this Burden-bearer Who did something new for you? Have you accepted the fact that Christ "borrows" to accomplish His purposes? What does He want from you, and are you surrendering it readily to Him?

Ye Should Do As I Have Done to You

John 13:2–17

Introduction:
People say, "The Bible is so hard to understand." Actually, the Bible isn't nearly as difficult to understand as it is to practice!

I. **I know what happened when Christ washed their feet.**
   A. Time sequence is not completely clear.
      1. It was right after entering upper room.
      2. It was prior to observance of last supper.
   B. Fits with custom/culture of time.
      1. Everything needful was on hand.
      2. He waited to see if anyone else would respond.
   C. Christ removed his garments (v. 4).
      1. Became clothed like a slave.
      2. Went about washing disciples' feet.
   D. Got into controversy with Peter (vv. 6–10).
      1. Peter balked at Christ washing his feet.
      2. Peter had no interest in washing anyone's feet.
   E. He explained to them what He had done (vv. 12–17).
      1. Gave spiritual information.
      2. Presented His action as an example to be followed.

II. **I know what was involved when He washed their feet.**
   A. Theological truth: He was showing humility and teaching about His humiliation.
      1. He did so knowingly (vv. 2–3).
         a. Judas was there—Christ knew what he would do.
         b. Christ had full understanding of His own status.
      2. He was picturing the full extent of His humiliation.
   B. Living truth: This was not something unique in His ministry.
      1. He had constantly served them (Luke 22:27).
      2. This was totally in accord with why He had come.
   C. Practical truth: He was teaching them how they should act.
      1. Best teaching is through example.
      2. He was not establishing an ordinance.

III. I don't comprehend all implications of the incident.
A. I should do what needs to be done in regard to others.
  1. Has to do with my spirit.
  2. This is what made the Samaritan good.
B. Nothing to be done for others is beneath my dignity.
  1. Hard to describe lowliness of footwashing.
  2. Test is not in the task but in the need of the task.
C. I should have a realistic view of myself.
  1. He is much greater than I—if He did so, no reason for me not to do so.
  2. Shows how He viewed self-concept theology; twelve men at dinner; not one had a poor self-concept.
D. I should do what needs to be done regardless of those for whom I do it.
  1. It is easier to do things for friends and the worthy.
  2. He washed the feet of Judas, knowing fully what he planned to do shortly.
E. I should seek opportunities to serve others.
  1. This was fully in accord with His life.
  2. I can't be like Him without this aspect.
F. I should undertake service joyfully.
  1. My spirit determines my success.
  2. If I would be like Him, I will do so gladly.

Conclusion:

The facts and even the interpretation of the Bible are fairly simple. The practical implications become another matter. Footwashing must be the daily expression of the spirit of the child of God who wishes to pattern after His Savior. The Bible is indeed a tough book!

"Lord, Is It I?"

Mark 14:17–21

Introduction:
> After a service we might say:
> "The sermon has been preached."
> "The invitation has been given."
> "The people have responded."
> "The benediction has been pronounced."
> "The postlude is now playing."
> "Let us all go home."

At too many times in too many places, all those things could not be said. There is a missing element: "The people have responded." This passage throws some light on that issue.

I. **The Setting**
 A. Chronologically: the last night of the last week.
 B. Geographically: in the upper room.
 C. Sequentially: right after they sat down, before the meal, before the foot washing, before the last supper.

II. **The Statement ("One of you . . . shall betray me.")**
 A. Shows that Christ knew what would happen—shows intensity of His love and spirit.
 B. Why did He mention it to them?
  1. To the disciples so they wouldn't be surprised and so that the event would confirm their faith.
  2. To Judas: to startle and to give one last chance.

III. **The Sorrow ("And they began to be sorrowful . . .")**
 A. Troubled that He would be betrayed.
 B. Troubled that one of them would do it.
 C. Troubled that they were uncertain of which one would do it.

IV. **The Searching (". . . Is it I? and another said, Is it I?")**
 A. This is surprising.
  1. Period when disciples look bad; this is the best light they throw on themselves throughout week.
  2. The participation of Judas? Crass arrogance or to deflect suspicion. ("Possible for a hypocrite to go through the world not only undetected but unsuspected.")

B. It shows self-suspicion.
  1. It becomes a true disciple to be always suspicious of himself.
  2. "We know not how strongly we may be tempted, nor how far God may leave us to ourselves, and therefore, have reasons not to be highminded but to fear!"
  3. "Many whose consciences condemn them are very industrious to justify themselves before men."
C. It shows great sensitivity.
  1. They were more concerned about themselves than each other. (Because we know ourselves, we ought always to expect more evil from ourselves than from others—but we don't.)
  2. They trusted His words more than their own hearts.
     a. Said, "Is it I?" rather than, "It is not I!"
     b. This was a very heavy accusation laid on them.

V. **The Significance**
  A. Whole point of story is to teach us to not to trust ourselves and to ever examine ourselves before His Word.
  B. But we don't do so—why?
    1. Stubbornness—couldn't admit wrong if it were to be proved.
    2. Self-will—view no other way or viewpoint as worthy.
    3. Spiritual indifference—don't care enough to bother.
    4. Self-righteousness—can't imagine being wrong.

Conclusion:
This brings us back to the original issue. Why do we often refuse to respond to God's message? Because we sit in judgment on His Word or self-vindicate rather than asking, "Lord, is it I?" The disciples rarely looked better than here; we rarely look worse!

The Lord's Supper

1 Corinthians 11:23–34

Introduction:

We often preach on the meaning of the Lord's Supper, but we seldom look at the observance itself. Here are ten things about the communion service itself.

I. **The Essence of the Ordinance**
   A. Some view it as a sacrament—a means of grace.
   B. Actually an ordinance—something ordered of the Lord.
      1. "This do in remembrance of me" (v. 24).
      2. No additional grace, just blessing from obedience.

II. **The Relationship of the Ordinance**
   A. There are just two ordinances: baptism and communion.
   B. Note the differences.
      1. Baptism is done just once—symbolizes a one-time thing.
      2. Communion is a continuous thing—symbolizes a continuing need.
   C. Note complementary nature.
      1. Baptism represents entry to Christian life.
      2. Communion represents the progress of the Christian life.
      3. Both are essential.

III. **The Continuous Nature of the Ordinance**
   A. Perpetuity established—"This do in remembrance of me."
   B. God must think we need it.
      1. Knows our human nature.
      2. We are prone to forget, trust ourselves, etc.

IV. **The Elements of the Communion**
   A. The Nature of the elements.
      1. Material—something tangible.
      2. Common—among the most common items of that day.
   B. The Lessons of the elements.
      1. The reality of the things symbolized.
      2. The freedom of participation.
      3. The practicality of God's dealing with us.

V. The Personal Nature of the Ordinance
A. "Eat ye all of it"—an individual commandment.
B. No one else can partake for us.
  1. Each individual must participate on his own.
  2. Stresses the individual nature of our relationship to Christ.

VI. The Substitution in the Ordinance
A. Blood of grape replaces blood of animal.
B. Speaks of work Christ accomplished.
  1. Old covenant—"this do and live."
  2. New covenant—"live and do this."

VII. The Joyful Nature of the Ordinance
A. Observance begins with blessing and ends with hymn.
B. It is a solemnly joyful service.
  1. Solemnity in remembering His death.
  2. Joy in realizing effects (we begin somber, but we end joyfully).

VIII. The Perpetual Nature of the Ordinance
A. "This do"—do the same thing in remembrance of me.
B. Hearing much about changes in religion, etc.
  1. God evidently didn't envision any other way.
  2. Provided symbolic memorial for all time.

IX. The Deeper Symbolism of the Ordinance
A. Note two things:
  1. Body and blood separated—results in death.
  2. Bread—represents very essence of life.
B. Shows that we feed on His death for our sustenance.

X. The Examination of the Ordinance
A. By now plain that we tread on hallowed ground.
B. Accounts for serious admonitions regarding participation.
  1. Not something to be treated lightly or flippantly.
  2. Demands great seriousness.

Conclusion:
Communion should not be "added on" to a service. Communion provides time of personal self-search. Communion should be warm and deepening time.

Three Men on Their Deathbeds

Luke 23:39–43

Introduction:

Come with me back across the years to a hilltop outside the gates of Jerusalem. There three crude crosses loom grotesquely against a lowering sky. These wooden crosses serve as deathbeds for three condemned men. Let us silently draw near to see who they are and what they might say:

I. **The First Cross** (v. 39)
    A. Who hangs here?
        1. A malefactor—common criminal.
        2. One being punished justly (v. 41a).
    B. What does he say?
        1. Rhetorical statement of unbelief.
        2. Railing.
    C. What do the words reveal?
        1. An evil heart.
        2. A total misunderstanding of the Messiah.
        3. A complete unbelief.

II. **The Second Cross** (vv. 40–42)
    A. Who hangs here?
        1. Another common criminal.
        2. Being punished justly.
    B. What does he say?
        1. To the other thief (vv. 40–41).
           a. Rebuke.
           b. Testimony.
        2. To Christ.
           a. Request for help.
           b. Tremendous statement.
    C. What do these words reveal?
        1. Change.
        2. Recognition.
        3. Faith.

III. **The Middle Cross** (v. 43)
    A. Who hangs there?
        1. One who has done nothing amiss.
        2. One we know to be the Son of God.
    B. What does he say?
        1. Expression of help.
        2. Grants more than thief requests.

C.   What does it show?
1.   Nature of His work.
2.   Place of dead believer.
3.   Danger of deathbed decision.

Conclusion:
"Three men shared death upon a hill,
But only one man died;
The other two—
A thief and God Himself—
Made a rendezvous.
Three crosses still
Are borne up Calvary's hill.
Where sin still lift's them high;
Upon the one sag broken men
Who, cursing, die.
Another holds the praying thief,
Or those who, penitent as he,
Still find the Christ
Beside them on the tree."

The People at the Cross

Introduction:
   We have come a long way in time from that distant scene. We need to recreate that setting in our own minds today. Let's look at the people there at the cross. There is an interesting tie because each group has its modern counterparts.

I.   **The Mob: Mocking Scorn** (Matthew 27:39–40)
   A.   Setting:
       1.   Roman carnival atmosphere (v. 36—picnic?).
       2.   Vast crowd of shifting components.
   B.   Action:
       1.   Shouts of scorn.
       2.   It is not likely that we have all recorded.
       3.   Part of intense humiliation.
   C.   Counterparts today:
       1.   Ignorant masses.
       2.   Make no investigation—just dismiss with flippant unconcern.
       3.   Includes vast mass of people.

II.   **The Religious Leaders Blasphemous Scorn** (27:41–43)
   A.   Setting:
       1.   Superintendents of crucifixion.
       2.   Victors in a running battle.
   B.   Action:
       1.   Hurl charges and challenges.
       2.   Designed to show and sway the people.
       3.   Sorely tried Him (added to His suffering).
   C.   Counterparts today:
       1.   Religious leaders.
       2.   Deny claims of Christ and encourage others to do so.
       3.   Abandon truth in quest of "relevance."

III.   **The Thieves: Doubting Scorn—Saving Faith** (Luke 23:39–43)
   A.   Setting:
       1.   Criminals sentenced by Rome (own admission).
       2.   Men in their ultimate extremity.
   B.   Action:
       1.   One hurls curses and blame.
       2.   Other turns for help.
       3.   Both are confronted with final truth.

C. Counterpart today:
1. People don't hang on crosses, but they do reach extremity.
2. People in extremity react as the thieves to Christ.
3. Some are confirmed in death; some translated to life.

IV. The Women: Fearful Devotion (John 19:25)
A. Setting:
1. Three significant women stand here.
   a. Jesus' mother.
   b. Her cousin and mother of James.
   c. Mary Magdalene out of whom Christ had cast seven devils.
2. Each had a reason for being there.
B. Action:
1. Much they did not understand.
2. They were wrapped in fear.
3. They clung to what they knew—Christ.
C. Counterparts today:
1. There are many who do not understand all they should.
2. They manifest much fear.
3. They cling to Christ (develop idea of holding on even in the dark).

V. The Disciples: Frightened Flight (John 19:26–27)
A. Setting:
1. His seizure had been a terrible blow.
   a. They really didn't expect it.
   b. He had handled it in a way to cover them.
2. They were shattered and scattered.
B. Action:
1. Evidently cross had a magnetic attraction.
2. John was there, doubtlessly others.
3. Came close enough to communicate but scarred to death.
C. Counterparts today:
1. Many today follow Jesus fearfully.
2. Know Him but fear consequences of following.
3. Follow afar off and frequently deny.

VI. The Roman Soldiers: Convinced Converts (Mark 15:37–39)
A. Setting:
1. Roman soldiers in charge of entire situation.
2. Were doing their duty in a day which didn't question.

B. Action:
   1. They observed whole situation (likely not many others did).
   2. They were relatively impartial.
   3. They weighed the evidence and were convinced.
C. Counterparts today:
   1. There are those today who approach Christ impartially.
   2. There are those who weigh the full weight of evidence.
   3. There are those who come to the same conclusion.

VII. The Suffering Savior: Dying Grace
A. Setting:
   1. All centers around one person (all else incidental).
   2. His role is the dominant.
B. Action:
   1. Christ shows forgiveness (Luke 23:34).
   2. He shows concern (Luke 23:28–31; 23:43; John 19:26–27).
   3. He dies for mankind (John 19:30).
C. Counterparts today:
   1. For Him there is no counterpart.
   2. He still remains forgiving, caring, and paying for man's sins.
   3. Reaction to Him still crucial.

Conclusion:
What kind of person are you today?
Mocking without really knowing.
Blaspheming without really caring.
Doubting and rejecting in extremity.
Receiving in the midst of the malestrom.
Trusting in shadow and fear.
Following in quaking fearfulness.
Convinced by careful investigation.
Whatever your response—Christ is the answer. The one who comes out best is the Roman Centurion.

The Sufferings of Christ

Colossians 1:24

Introduction:

It would be difficult to over-stress the sufferings of Christ. The price He paid for our sin actually surpasses human explanation.

I. **What Christ Suffered** (Phil. 3:10)
   A. Crucifixion—but much more . . .
   B. Indifference of others.
   C. Human limitations.
   D. Misunderstandings.
   E. False accusations.
   F. Total rejection.

II. **The "Lack" in His Sufferings** (Col. 1:24)
   A. Meaning:
      1. God was satisfied. (Isa. 53:11)
      2. Christ's enemies were not—as far as they are concerned, there was more to go.
   B. Application:
      1. He is not here to suffer.
      2. His followers and servants must suffer what was (is) intended for Him.
   C. Truth—If you are not suffering some things because of your Christianity, you are not a spirit-filled believer.

III. **Is It Worth It?**
   A. Christ gave His life; can we not give something? (2 Cor. 5:15)
   B. We suffer for so many other things.
   C. It is but a moment. (1 Peter 5:10)
   D. The future glory is tied in with present suffering. (Rom. 8:17-18; 2 Tim. 2:12)

Conclusion:

There is no room for masochism here. This is suffering for doing what one deems right and proper.

The Seven Last Words

Introduction:

This is the season when we fix our attention on the cross of the Lord Jesus Christ. The dying words which He uttered there are of great significance to us; they are the last words of the greatest of all who have lived on earth.

I.   **The First Word—"The word of intercession"** (Luke 23:34)
  A. The reasons for the prayer:
    1. Tells why He was dying.
    2. Reveals His character.
    3. Provides a perfect example for disciples.
    4. Fulfills prophecy.
  B. The objects of the prayer:
    1. The soldiers who nailed them there.
    2. The Jews who condemned Him to be nailed there.
    3. All who have in any way contributed to the sin load which brought Him to the cross.
  C. The answers to the prayer:
    1. Soldiers and Jews spared then and there.
    2. Jewish nation given forty years of grace to receive the great message.
    3. All people were forgiven; people must simply receive the forgiveness which has already been provided.

II. **The Second Word—"The word of compassion"** (Luke 23:39–43)
  A. Note the penitent thief:
    1. His rebuke of the other thief and his request of Christ reveal a change in heart.
    2. He reveals his recognition of his own guilt.
    3. He expresses all he knows in a cry of faith.
  B. Note Christ's reaction:
    1. Expresses help—beyond thief's request.
    2. Reveals the nature of His work.
    3. Shows the place of the dead believer.
  C. Note the caution:
    1. Many have used this to excuse procrastination.
    2. Notice that two came to deathbeds: one repented; one did not repent.
    3. God's grace is shown, but think of how much is missed.

III. The Third Word—"The word of dying concern" (John 19:25–27)
   A. Mary is suffering there.
      1. Had been predicted by Simeon.
      2. Is fulfilled now as she shares in His suffering and loses her beloved son.
   B. Christ singles her out for attention.
      1. Calls her "woman."
         a. Desire to spare her hurt of "mother."
         b. Imparts proper perspective—she would have to be saved like anyone else.
      2. Turns her over to John.
   C. Christ demonstrates:
      1. Proper family regard.
      2. Deep concern for others (half of His last words are concerned with others).

IV. The Fourth Word—"The word of abandonment" (Mark 15:34)
   A. Shows the extent of His sufferings:
      1. Enormous physical agony.
      2. Silence of God and nature—God has actually turned away from Him.
   B. Shows the cause of His suffering:
      1. Christ has been made sin for us.
      2. All of human sin has been poured out on Him.

V. The Fifth Word—"The word of personal need" (John 19:28)
   A. This word shows the extent of His physical suffering.
      1. Had become intense to point of exhaustion.
      2. Not spoken until words of concern for others is spoken.
   B. This word demonstrates Christ's complete humanity.
      1. As Very God He felt separation from God.
      2. As Very Man He felt intense human suffering.
      3. The fact of this humanity makes His work valid for us.
   C. This word shows the fulfillment of prophecy.
      1. Predicted in Psalm 22:15; 69:21b.
      2. This authenticates Christ.

VI. The Sixth Word—"The word of completion" (John 19:30)
   A. The physical suffering of Christ.
      1. This was part of the plan of God.
      2. Was so that we might never have to suffer.
   B. The humiliation of Christ.
      1. Involved in His coming from Glory (Phil. 2).
      2. Trace steps.

C. The whole program of the Old Testament.
   1. The gap-bridging insititutions of the Old Testament were no longer necessary nor valid.
   2. Rent in veil of temple indicated this.
D. The word of redemption.
   1. Center of work of redemption is Cross.
   2. This means:
      a. God and man reconciled.
      b. Conflict of ages already won.
      c. Door open to salvation to all.
      d. Responsibility placed on individual.

VII. The Seventh Word—"The word of conclusion" (Luke 23:46)
A. Note that He dismisses His spirit.
   1. His death is different from any other.
   2. His death is absolutely voluntary—no one else (including God) takes His life.
B. This voluntary element is absolutely essential.
   1. It had to be voluntary for God to be just.
   2. It had to be voluntary for God to be God (people can't kill God).
   3. It had to be voluntary to display fully His love.

Conclusion:
The seven words give us a full-orbed picture of Christ: His love, His life, His death, His purpose. Do you know Him as your Savior and Lord?

Risen and Alive

Matthew 28:6

Introduction:

This byword of the early Christians "He is not here: for He is risen," had tremendous meaning to them. It still means much to us. Some thoughts on what it means that He is risen and alive forevermore.

I.   **Life Is Worth Living**
   A.   It has meaning.
   B.   It makes sense.
   C.   It has ultimate worth.

II. **Prayer Has a Point**
   A.   We are repeatedly commanded to go through Christ.
   B.   His intervention is promised to us.
   C.   His resurrection is necessary to make these things meaningful.

III. **The Future Can Be Faced**
   A.   God knows the future.
   B.   He has promised His presence through the person of His Son.
   C.   His resurrection assures His presence.

IV. **Death Can Be Handled**
   A.   Life's most difficult subject.
   B.   It can be handled by the Christian.
   C.   We can handle it because He handled it for us.

V.   **Eternity Can Be Sure**
   A.   We can know for sure.
   B.   Involves first-fruit principle.
   C.   Are you sure? On what basis?

Conclusion:

He is risen and He is alive for evermore. That has many meanings. Does it mean anything to you? Will you do something about it?

The Word of Intercession
Luke 23:34

Introduction:
The trial was over, the procession had wended its weary way to Calvary's hill. The cross was stretched out, and the Lord laid upon it; the nails pounded, and the cross dropped into the ground. Lifting His eyes to heaven, He speaks:

I. **Why Did Christ Pray This Prayer?**
    A. Expresses His essential reason for dying.
        1. Dying that all might be forgiven.
        2. Prayer expresses basis of Cross.
    B. Reveals His character.
        1. Loving compassion upon those apart.
        2. Thoughts always for others.
    C. Provides disciples with example.
        1. Taught by precept and example.
        2. Becomes example for us.
    D. It was a fulfillment of a prophecy.
        1. Isaiah 53:12.
        2. This provides another in the great chain of prophecy.

II. **For Whom Was He Praying**
    A. The immediate subjects.
        1. Had just been nailed to the cross.
        2. Would comprehend the soldiers at this point.
    B. The further extension.
        1. Death was caused by the demand of national pride.
        2. Comprehends the Jewish nation.
    C. The ultimate extension.
        1. The real sin is taking place here.
            a. Note the crucifixion—"For they know not what they do."
            b. Sin is rejection of Son of God.
        2. Thus it extends to everyone.
            a. Anyone who rejects Christ is guilty of the same sin Christ asks to have forgiven.
            b. Had we been there, we would have done the same thing no doubt.

III. **Was the Prayer Answered?**
    A. Physically.
        1. Soldiers and Jews spared.
        2. Jerusalem and Jewish nation spared.

B. Spiritually.
   1. Why He was dying.
      a. All was forgiven in His death.
      b. Made it plain that even those actually participating were pardoned.
   2. The Father did forgive.
      a. Only some accepted the proffered salvation.
      b. You have already been forgiven the sin of rejecting Christ if you will just stop doing it now.

Conclusion:

"Father, forgive them . . ." is an expression of His heart. Have you accepted His forgiveness?

Forsaken of the Father

Mark 15:34

Introduction:

Of all the mysteries in the world and the Word there is none like the crucifixion. The details defy explanation, the writers maintain a hush, and history is silent. There is a deeper mystery in the midst of mystery as this is the time when Christ was made sin. At this point the Gospel writers grow absolutely silent, and the only record we have of what took place is the words of Christ at the close of this period—"MY GOD, MY GOD, WHY HAST THOU FORSAKEN ME?"

I. **The Extent of the Suffering**
   - A. Great physical agony up to now.
      1. Pressure
      2. Lack of sleep
      3. Buffeting
      4. Crown of thorns
      5. Whipping
      6. Bearing cross (failure shows extent of physical suffering)
      7. Actual crucifixion
   - B. All this is as a pin-prick or bruise compared with what took place during this period of silence.

II. **The Cause of the Suffering**
   - A. Christ here is made sin for us.
      1. Initial personal contact with sin.
      2. All of human sin poured out on Him.
   - B. Sin is incomprehensible in scope.
      1. All sin involved in crucifixion was heaped on Him.
      2. Take a depraved mind and allow it to course freely through the deepest imaginable pit of debasement and still the picture of what He bore is not complete.

III. **The Nature of the Suffering**
   - A. Separation from the Father
      1. Words are true.
      2. Involves separation for . . .
         a. He was "in the beginning with God."
         b. He had said, "I and the Father are One."
         c. He had known a human and an eternal lifetime of communion with God.

B. Cause of the separation
  1. Christ bore sin.
  2. Holy God can't look on sin.
  3. Had to turn back on Son.
C. Separation broke . . .
  1. Love
  2. Care
  3. Communion

Conclusion:

"He was made sin for us . . . that we might be righteousness . . ." His suffering is never appropriated, however, until we accept Him. "He died that they which live . . . should live unto Him." His suffering is never appreciated until we begin to live for Him in real dedication.

I Thirst

John 19:28

Introduction:

Christ said, "I thirst." He thus revealed both His true humanity and the extent of His suffering.

I. **Its Interesting Sequence**
   A. Their organization:
      1. Three statements concerned with others.
      2. Three statements concerned with redemption.
      3. One statement of conclusion.
   B. Their demonstration:
      1. Concern first of all with others.
      2. Concern for self is primarily in the spiritual.
      3. When all else is accomplished, He speaks of self.

II. **Its Essential Demonstration**
   A. Reason for the word.
      1. Doesn't speak just for own comfort.
      2. Would teach us something here.
   B. Demonstrates extent of physical sufferings.
      1. Thirst reveals exhaustion.
      2. Must be intense to make Christ cry out.
   C. Demonstrates His complete humanity.
      1. Connected with last word.
      2. Important for atonement.
   D. Demonstration of voluntary nature of atonement.
      1. Could have stopped it at any point.
      2. Allowed it to go all the way—did not have to die, Christ chose to die.

III. **Its Purposed Result**
   A. What it was.
      1. To fulfill predictive prophecy.
      2. Not just a statement to answer a previously made predictive statement.
   B. The fulfillment of prediction.
      1. The prophecy (Ps. 22:15; 69:21b)
      2. The fulfillment.
   C. The evidences of fulfilled prophecy.
      1. Men try to obliterate this.

2. The reason.
   a. Fulfilled predictions authenticate Christ.
   b. Fulfilled predictions preclude any attempts to tear apart inspiration.
3. The truth.
   a. These predictions can't be done away with.
   b. The things those who oppose Him fear then happen.

Conclusion:

As we hear Him say, "I thirst," it should make us realize again what He suffered and realize again that it was for us He suffered. It should also make us see the fulfillment of prophecy (predicition) and value the Word even more highly.

The Word of Conclusion
Luke 23:46

Introduction:
"My God, My God"—expresses the depth of His suffering. "It is finished"—expresses the completion of His suffering, of His death, and of His atoning work. "Father . . ."—speaks again to the Father, their fellowship restored.

I. **Interesting Action**
    A. Fellowship was restored.
    B. Christ cries with a loud voice.
        1. Physical strength left.
        2. Did not die of natural causes.
    C. Entrusts spirit to God's care.
    D. He "dismisses" His spirit.

II. **Potent Demonstration**
    A. His death was different from any other.
        1. No one else dismisses the spirit.
        2. Even with a suicide, it is "taken."
    B. His death is absolutely voluntary.
        1. It is not taken by crucifiers.
        2. Not by natural causes.
        3. Spirit not taken by God.
        4. This thing is completely in His own control.

III. **Essential Importance**
    A. Volition essential to divine justice.
        1. Justice attribute of God.
        2. Sin must be punished.
        3. Christ is substitute.
        4. Christ, the innocent, must *voluntarily* die to protect the justice of God.
    B. Volition essential to His deity.
        1. Men can't kill God.
        2. Physical suffering can't kill God.
        3. Christ was fully in control right up to the end.
    C. Volition essential to full display of His love.
        1. Love was shown by His death.
        2. Fact that He could have stopped was indicated by fact that He chose to proceed.
        3. How we need to be like Him in the extent of our love for others and the lost.

Conclusion:

The seventh word assures us that His death was truly voluntary. This is the just death of the divine Son of God showing His great love for all sinners.

'Tis Done, the Great Transaction's Done

John 19:30

Introduction:

We press toward the close of the deepest of mystery, the center of revelation, a divine paradox. Christ utters yet another word, probably in a loud voice, "It is finished." Yet it stands as a cryptic conundrum until we ask a particular pertinent question to unlock its secrets. What is finished? The answers come quick and varied.

I. **The Humiliation of Christ**
    A. Meaning: "His continuing self-renunciation which takes place out of the voluntary submission of self."
    B. The steps:
        1. Began when the purposes of redemption were set in eternity past.
        2. Leaving heaven for earth.
        3. Laying aside of glory.
        4. Laying aside divine prerogatives.
        5. Suffering at the hands of men.
        6. Separation from God.
        7. Burial (exaltation begins at resurrection).
    C. Reasons for the humiliation.
        1. That He might become sin for us.
        2. That we might not have to experience this.

II. **The Physical Sufferings of Christ**
    A. The possibility of suffering in Christ.
        1. Human nature suffered like any other would.
        2. Divine nature suffered through contact with the instruments of sin (Heb. 12:3).
    B. The plan of God.
        1. This is no mistake (plainly predicted in Isaiah).
        2. Divinely ordained (Hebrews 2:10).
    C. The purpose of the sufferings.
        1. It was absolutely necessary for substitution.
        2. So that we will never have to suffer the pain of separation from God.

III. **The Whole Program of the Old Testament**
    A. Basis of that program.
        1. Gulf between man and God.
        2. Distant man—inaccessible God.

B. Operation of that program—sacrificial system.
C. The termination of that program.
   1. Old Testament system was terminated.
   2. Because—doorway to God open through the work of Christ.
   3. It was symbolized by rending veil of temple.
   4. Benefit—we may go directly to God without any intermediary at all.

IV. The Work of Redemption
A. The center of the work of redemption is the Cross.
   1. We must always keep the Cross and redemption related.
   2. The Cross is redemption.
B. Is the work really finished?
   1. There are things yet to transpire.
   2. With this much done, successful completion is an absolute necessity and certainty.
C. The meaning of the work that was completed.
   1. Man and God are reconciled.
   2. The conflict of the ages is won.
   3. The door is open to salvation.
   4. Responsibility is placed upon you.

Conclusion:

It is finished! What is finished? His physical suffering for us. His humiliation for us. The Old Testament program for us. The work of redemption for us. "For me He died, for me He lives, and everlasting life and light He freely gives."

Is There Life After Life?

Luke 16:19–31

Introduction:

When a society begins to decay and decline, it begins to lose hope. This reflects in culture and art through realism, harshness, and surrealism. It begins to show up in preoccupation with inevitabilities. Our decaying, declining society is rapidly becoming totally preoccupied with death.

I. **The Findings**
   A. People quoted:
      1. Those who have experienced clinical death
      2. "Life after life" experiences
   B. Experiences:
      1. Basically they are uniform
      2. Included: Sense of euphoria; open freedom; review of life's events, etc.; no desire to return, etc.
   C. Results:
      1. None were anxious to return.
      2. None now fears death at all.

II. **The Fiction**
   A. Definition of death crucial:
      1. Medical (vital signs, brain waves, heartbeat, etc.)
      2. Actual—Separation of soul and body
   B. Meaning:
      1. All cases were examples of clinical death, not actual death.
      2. No one has actually returned from the dead.
   C. Result:
      1. Confusion reigns supreme.
      2. We are lacking in essential evidence.

III. **The Facts**
   A. Just one has come back from actual death and told about it.
      1. That one is Jesus Christ.
      2. New Testament contains record He has given.
   B. Much teaching in story He gave (Luke 16:19–31).
      1. There is something (life) after death.
      2. Life after death is in one of two locations.
      3. Hell is real and awful.
      4. There is no second chance after death.

     5. There is no exchange of places after death (v. 26).
     6. Stations here and hereafter are not related.
     7. Position there is determined by decisions now.
  C. No evidence should be allowed to contradict His.
     1. He taught about it with divine knowledge.
     2. He taught as one who had been there and back.

IV. The Future
  A. We must face inevitability of death.
     1. Difference between facing and being preoccupied with death.
     2. Total inescapability.
  B. We must make a decision regarding it.
     1. Bible says "born again" is necessary to see heaven.
     2. Explain "born again."
  C. Your decision today may affect your destiny.
     1. May never be in right place again.
     2. You surely make a decision today.

Conclusion:

Don't get taken in by something untrue regarding life after death. Take the Word and the record of the only One who has ever come back and told of it.

A Voice from the Dead

Luke 16:19–31

Introduction:

There is much interest in the Shroud of Turin and the sighting of Noah's ark. Neither has been confirmed. We think, "if only we could find something like that." We think finding something like that would confirm the Bible and make people believe. Unfortunately, such is not the case.

I. **If only someone could return from the dead . . .**
   A. Trace the story in the text.
   B. Rich man wanted someone sent back from the dead to warn his brothers of their potential destiny.
   C. We sometimes think—if only there were something to confirm the truths of Scripture.

II. **If someone could return from the dead, it would be of no avail.**
   A. Simple statement of Jesus (v. 31).
   B. Clear evidence statement is correct.
      1. God spoke at Sinai—made little difference.
      2. Prophets performed mighty miracles—only few believed.
      3. Christ came as the Son of God—they crucified Him.
      4. Lazarus arose from the dead—hardened opposition (Jn. 12:10).
      5. Christ rose from dead—soldier witnesses lied.

III. **Return from the dead would be of no avail for good reasons.**
   A. Men have come back from the dead.
      1. No indication that any ever said a word about it.
      2. No indication it had any effect whatever on others.
   B. Whole idea questions perfection of God.
      1. If there were way to make Gospel more effective, God would have already done it.
      2. What God has already given must be the best way.
   C. God has made other provision.
      1. "Moses and the Prophets" refers to the Bible.
      2. God has already told us what we need to know.
         a. "Holy Scripture is so perfect, so complete, that it cannot want the supplement of any declaration concerning a future state."

b. All you need to know about the future is already in the Bible.
3. The Bible tells us more than we like to admit.
   a. "If you don't know the difference between right and wrong from reading the Bible, you would not know it should a spirit show it to you."
   b. If you don't know the road to heaven and to hell from the Bible, you will not know it from anything else.
4. There is other evidence readily available.
   a. The influence of the Gospel on society.
   b. The spectacle of a changed life.
   c. The observation of people passing through deep waters successfully.
5. People don't fail to believe because of want of truth but because of want of heart to believe the truth (Rom. 10:8–10).
6. Miracles may make people wonder, but they will not make people believe.

Conclusion:

A voice from the dead would be of no avail because you need nothing else. Act now; don't wait until it is too late.

Vain Seeking

Luke 24:1–6

Introduction:

Easter morning must have been amazing for the disciples. They had missed the message and must have been awed by the reality of it all. They received a rebuke: "Why seek ye the living among the dead?" They heard the correction: "He is risen *as He said*." Their seeking was vain! It is easy to be critical of them, but people today are still vain seeking.

I. **Seeking Him in Places He Cannot Be Found**
    A. In religion.
        1. Probably nothing has done more to hide Christ than organized religion.
        2. If He is found in much Christianity, it is accidental.
    B. In philosophy.
        1. The whole tone of modern philosophy is humanistic.
        2. There is no room for Christ because it is too full of human values.
    C. In legalism.
        1. Through meeting and keeping terms of the law.
        2. Anything that makes performance necessary to salvation is incorrect because it misses point of resurrection.

II. **Seeking Him Among People Where He Cannot Be Found**
    A. The gloomy and despairing.
        1. If He is found here, it should not be so.
        2. No room for gloom and despair among His people.
    B. The doubting and unsure.
        1. If Job could say, "I know that my redeemer liveth," how much more should we (Job 19:25).
        2. How sad to live life unsure of the things that pertain to Him.
    C. The habitually sinning.
        1. Salvation makes a change; where there is not change, there must be a question of salvation.
        2. He should not be found among those who constantly practice sin.
    D. The worldly.
        1. "If ye then be risen with Christ . . ."
        2. He should not be found among those unwilling to renounce the world.

III. Seeking Him in Ways in Which He Cannot Be Found
    A. Ritualism.
        1. No religious observance leads to Christ.
        2. No religious observance necessary to come to Him.
    B. Self-effort.
        1. Includes all forms of religious observance and self-help philosophies.
        2. No amount of self-effort can avail in finding Him.
    C. Morality.
        1. Neither doing good or refraining from doing bad.
        2. There is no moral standard—even a hypothetical one—adequate to reach Him.

Conclusion:

Then how or where is He found? He is found directly; He is found by faith; He is found in prayer. "Why seek ye the living among the dead?"

The "He" Who Is Risen

Luke 24:36–49

Introduction:

Students often suffer anxiety before school begins. They wonder what the teacher is like. We often wonder what people are really like out of the public eye. This incident provides a special insight into Christ. The risen Christ was like the living Christ; since He is the same, He is today what He was then.

I. **He is concerned about peace** (v. 36)
   A. It was shown in this meeting.
      1. They had much to be upset about.
      2. His first words were, "peace be unto you."
   B. This continues to be His message.
      1. It is never His purpose for His people to be upset.
         a. He takes no delight in the distresses of His people.
         b. He desires us to find peace in the midst of strife.
      2. When we are filled with strife, the cause is within us.
      3. Remember John 14:27.

II. **He is concerned about faith** (vv. 38–39, 41–43)
   A. Christ questions, "Why are ye troubled and why do thoughts arise in your hearts?" ("... doubts arise in your minds") (vv. 38–39).
      1. He challenges their unbelief.
      2. He does so in unique way.
         a. Before His ascension, Christ had forbidden Mary to touch Him.
         b. Now He encourages Thomas to do so.
         c. He did whatever was necessary to encourage their faith.
   B. He confronts their continued unbelief (41–43).
      1. It seems to make difference here (unbelief of confusion).
      2. He gives them evidence to go on.
         a. He eats here—not for His need but for theirs.
         b. He shows His great patience with people.
   C. He still challenges doubt and demands belief.
      1. He rebukes unbelief and seeks to eliminate it.
      2. He encourages faith in every possible way (gives us many "signs along the way").

III. He is concerned about intimate fellowship (vv. 40, 43)
- A. He allows real intimacy.
  1. He allows touch.
  2. He shows His hands and feet.
- B. He still desires intimacy with His people.
  1. He pushes us to fellowship with Him.
  2. He hears our griefs.
  3. He indulges our infirmities (regards our cry about a sword in our bones when it is nothing more than a thorn in our flesh).
  4. He is a brother born for our every adversity.

IV. He is concerned about Scripture (vv. 44–45)
- A. He exalts the Scripture, insists it must be kept entirely.
  1. Jesus always shows a high view of Scripture.
  2. Our views of Scripture should be based on His view.
- B. He desires us to have a high view of Scripture now.
  1. The Bible must be in the foreground.
  2. The Bible must be a practical part of our lives.

V. He is concerned about the souls of all people (vv. 46–49)
- A. Christ gives a clear commandment.
  1. Reason for His suffering—forgiveness for sin.
  2. That message must be preached to everyone.
  3. Disciples given specific responsibility.
  4. Promise of Holy Spirit's help given.
- B. Christ is still interested in the salvation of mankind.
  1. The missionary spirit is the spirit of Christ.
  2. He is concerned with each individual.

Conclusion:

It is easy to know what Christ was like as we have much recorded about Him such as this incident. We can summarize by saying that He was concerned about people. If you know Him, you can't be like Him without concern for people. If you don't know Him, that is the starting point.

Because He Lives

1 Corinthians 15:12–19; John 14:19

Introduction:

There is an emphasis on life and new life at Easter. Because He lives! What difference does it make? Well, because He lives . . .

I. **Life is worth living.**
    A. It has meaning.
        1. His death and resurrection confirm His message.
        2. His message gives life meaning.
    B. It makes sense.
        1. His resurrection ties us in to another world.
        2. Necessary for life to make sense.
    C. It has ultimate worth.
        1. "If in this life only . . ."
        2. Life has eternal value.

II. **Prayer has a point.**
    A. Repeatedly commanded to go through Him (John 15:16).
        1. "His Name" a key issue in prayer.
        2. He is only One we are to go through (1 Tim. 2:5; Matt. 23:9).
    B. His intervention for us is promised.
        1. He prays for us.
        2. He beseeches the Father on our behalf.
    C. His resurrection validates His promises.
        1. Explain validation.
        2. If He is not risen, all is empty.

III. **The future can be faced.**
    A. God knows the future.
        1. There are no surprises to Him.
        2. All is laid out in advance.
    B. He has promised His presence in the Person of Christ.
        1. He is with us to the end.
        2. It means future makes no difference.
    C. His life allows His presence.
        1. If He stayed dead, there is no present presence.
        2. Because He lives, He is with us.

IV. Death can be handled.
A. Life's most difficult subject.
1. People are fascinated by it.
2. Either cower or swagger.
B. Can be handled by Christian.
1. Own death.
2. Others near us.
C. We can handle because He handled it.
1. Know it can be handled.
2. Let Him do it for us.

V. Eternity can be sure.
A. We can know.
1. There is so much "hope and guess."
2. 1 John 5:17—What we have—eternal life.
B. Involves first-fruit principle.
1. First-fruits guaranteed remainder.
2. He was the down-payment.
C. Are you sure?
1. On what basis?
2. Why not?

Conclusion:
Because He lives many things are true, and He does live! Will you live because He lives?